The 401(k) Road Map

A Fiduciary's Guide to
401(k) Strategy

Peter Weitz

BALBOA.
PRESS

A DIVISION OF HAY HOUSE

Balboa Press books may be ordered through booksellers or by contacting:

Balboa Press
A Division of Hay House
1663 Liberty Drive
Bloomington, IN 47403
www.balboapress.com
1 (877) 407-4847

Because of the dynamic nature of the Internet, any web addresses or
links contained in this book may have changed since publication and
may no longer be valid. The views expressed in this work are solely those
of the author and do not necessarily reflect the views of the publisher,
and the publisher hereby disclaims any responsibility for them.

Print information available on the last page.

ISBN: 978-1-5043-7071-4 (sc)
ISBN: 978-1-5043-7072-1 (e)

Balboa Press rev. date: 04/12/2018

Disclaimer

This book has been written by Peter Weitz. This book is for information and illustrative purposes only and does not purport to show actual results. It is not, and should not be regarded as investment advice or as a recommendation regarding any individual security or course of action. Opinions expressed herein are current opinions as of the date appearing in this material only and are subject to change without notice. Reasonable people may disagree about the opinions expressed herein. In the event, any of the assumptions used herein do not prove to be true, results are likely to vary substantially. All investments entail risks. There is no guarantee that investment strategies will achieve the desired results under all market conditions and each investor should evaluate its ability to invest for a long term especially during periods of a market downturn. No representation is being made that any account, product, or strategy will or is likely to achieve profits, losses, or results like those discussed, if any. No part of this document may be reproduced in any manner, in whole or in part, without the prior written permission of Peter Weitz, other than to your employees. This book is provided with the understanding that with respect to the material provided herein, that you will make your own independent decision with respect to any course of action in connection herewith and as to whether such course of action is appropriate or proper based on your own judgment, and that you are capable of understanding and assessing the merits of a course of action. Peter Weitz does not purport to and does not, in any fashion, provide tax, accounting, actuarial, recordkeeping, legal, or any related services. You may not rely on the statements contained herein. Peter Weitz shall not have any liability for any damages of any kind whatsoever relating to this material. You should consult your advisors with respect to these areas. By reading this material, you acknowledge, understand and accept the foregoing.

Contents

Prologue

As the Chief Executive Officer of a money management firm that oversees and is responsible for hundreds of millions of dollars in public and private funds, I am generally well-versed in what my fiduciary, regulatory and statutory obligations are - if anyone should understand the nitty gritty of the investment world, it should be someone like me. However, it took a fortuitous meeting with Peter Weitz to wake me up and make me realize 401(k) plans were a different beast and well beyond my experience. After five minutes with Peter I quickly realized we needed specialized help. I didn't even know we had or needed an advisor on our 401(k) plan, but after meeting Peter the need was instantly obvious.

This is a competitive world, and we work in a competitive industry, so keeping employees happy should be at the forefront of every manager's plan. Having a properly designed 401(k) plan is an important addition to a competitive employee benefit package. And if you are like us, with highly specialized 401(k) plan needs, deferred compensation plans, and specific high level compensation and benefit needs, plan specialists like Peter are as important to our business as a good portfolio manager is to managing a mutual fund.

This book will highlight the issues that I was not aware of until I met Peter, and should give you a solid base of understanding as to what your requirements are as a fiduciary. Even though I know Peter personally and he is a valued consultant to my organization, I look forward to learning more about his processes and being able to use this book for reference in the future.

Peter DeCaprio
Chief Executive Officer
Crow Point Partners
25 Recreation Park Drive, Suite 110
Hingham, MA 02043

Chapter One

YOU are a Fiduciary

Since you have opened the first page of this book, it is highly likely are you are a Fiduciary. As a historical reference, The Employee Retirement Income Security Act (ERISA) enacted in 1974 is a federal law that sets minimum standards for defined benefit and defined contribution plans. It also provides the rules on the federal income taxation of many types of transactions associated with employee benefit plans.[1] ERISA is designed to protect the interests of employee benefit plan participants and their beneficiaries by:

- Requiring the disclosure of financial and other information concerning the plan to beneficiaries;
- Establishing standards of conduct for plan fiduciaries;
- Provide for appropriate remedies and access to the courts.

ERISA is the entity that regulates the rules of employee benefit plans, which are contained in the Internal revenue code and in ERISA itself. For the moment, let me focus on the second bullet point above. ERISA establishes standards of conduct for those who manage an employee benefit plan and its assets, called fiduciaries. However, let me be clear as to what the implication of fiduciary means. It is not simply a title or role. It is instead defined by the actual function that is performed. In fact, many of the elements involved in managing a 401(k) plan, by function, make the person performing those actions a fiduciary regardless of if they carry the title or not.

A "named fiduciary" refers to a person who has the ultimate control or authority over any decision relating to plan assets. Consider this person the Chief Executive Officer of the plan with total authority to appoint and give instructions to the plan trustee whose job is to accept funds, manage them prudently and distribute them to beneficiaries. In most cases, the named fiduciary will be either the employer, an officer of the employer, or an authorized appointee based upon a rule written in the plan document. While the "named fiduciary" is the authorized person having control over the plan operations, plan fiduciaries will also include investment advisors, anyone exercising discretion in the administration of the plan, and all members of the investment committee (more on this in a later chapter).

So, who cares? Why am I devoting the first chapter of this book on the boring role of a fiduciary? Because a fiduciary has significant responsibilities and standards of conduct that must be followed. Their role is to act in the best interests of the plan *participant* and not in the best interests of the corporation for which they are employed.

Fiduciaries must act with prudence, which often requires expertise beyond their own skill set. Thus, they are empowered to hire third party skilled professionals to assist with issues related to the management of the retirement plan such as asset allocation and investment selection. More importantly, under ERISA, the fiduciaries are required to have a process. In 2008, The Supreme Court overturned a lower court ruling in a landmark case that essentially created a significant checks and balances of responsibilities for fiduciaries. In LaRue v. DeWolff, Boberg & Associates, The

Supreme Court ruled that individual participants can now sue the trustees of a 401(k) plan based specifically on process and lack thereof. Let me repeat that again. Individual participants can now sue the trustees of a 401(k) plan based specifically on process.

> Aside: Make the distinction that process does not involve performance. It has been determined in the courts that trustees of a plan cannot be sued due to lack of performance of an investment, as no individual has a crystal ball to guarantee a return on investment.

In this case, the trustees of the plan failed to monitor the costs of both the service providers and the investment alternatives, and failed to have any evaluative criteria or "road map" as to how and how often they would evaluate the service providers and investment alternatives.

In early 2012 and because of this case, plan fiduciaries and sponsors began to receive information disclosing fees to administer the plan and to manage the investments in the plan. It was at this point that sponsors and Trustees were given the additional responsibility of insuring that all plan fees are reasonable and there are no conflicts of interest with any plan service providers, as well as ensure that any of the information that must be furnished to plan participants and beneficiaries is provided in a timely manner. It was further their responsibility to report any changes to the fee structure of the plan to all participants in a timely manner. Interestingly though, a survey conducted by Mr. Burton G. Malkiel, Professor of Economics, Emeritus, and a Senior Economist at Princeton University, found that many full-time employed baby boomers do not have a clear understanding of the fees they are paying in their retirement accounts. When asked what they pay in retirement account fees, 46 percent believed that they do not pay any fees at all. A further 19 percent suggest that their fees are less than 0.5 percent. Only 4 percent of those surveyed believe they pay over 2 percent in retirement account fees. [2] LaRue proved to the court that his company had no process, did not have any idea what the fees were inside of his retirement plan, and no benchmarks to determine whether the plan costs were reasonable.

As a further result of this landmark case, lawyers have begun feasting on the very large 401(k) plans with extremely successful outcomes. Whether you are aware of this or not, it is becoming a major issue and the mounting lawsuits are the proof!

Fiduciaries breaching their duties under ERISA, including a failure to comply with the 2012 disclosure rules, may be personally liable to replace any losses to the plan or restore any profits made through improper use of the plan's assets because of the breach. Simply stated an individual participant can bring civil action against a fiduciary for failure to comply with the new disclosures.

Scary, isn't it? But there's more to this story. With responsibility comes liability. As mentioned earlier, violations to the basic standards of conduct are a personal liability and not a corporate one. Thus, a failure by a covered service provider to provide the proper and timely disclosures will result in a prohibited transaction under ERISA and the Internal Revenue Code. This means that the fiduciary could be subject to excise taxes and must correct the violation, which may mean refunding the investment manager's compensation plus interest on that amount. In addition, if the Department of Labor ("DOL") recovers the compensation for the plan through either a settlement agreement or a court order, an additional 20 percent penalty may be imposed. [3]

In a recent presentation that I made to a group of Chief Financial Officers I began my presentation by stating that up until now they prioritized their day to day activities with line items like rent, payroll, debt and revenue being the at the top of the list and the 401(k) not even cracking top 100 of the priority list. With the recent changes to the regulations, this ranking in the priority list will absolutely have to change. If the 401(k) plan and the fiduciary responsibility associated with it are not at least in the top 10 of priorities for a Chief Financial Officer to think about, then they are going to be shell shocked when the DOL comes calling with an audit, as well as the potentially significant fines associated with non-compliance that were never budgeted for.

Still scared? There's more. Employers are becoming aware that the feds are aggressively investigating company-sponsored 401(k) plans for compliance issues. So, it is alarming to find out that the clear majority of plans the DOL looked at last year ran afoul of ERISA in some way. Let me outline some data points for you to chew on:

- *75% of the 401k plans* audited by the DOL in 2014 resulted in plan sponsors being fined, penalized or forced to make reimbursements for plan errors.
- The average fine last year was $600,000 per plan. That's a jump of nearly $150K from four years ago.
- 88 individuals — from plan officials to corporate officers to service providers — were criminally indicted for 401k offenses, per the DOL[3]

If a plan is subject to ERISA, the DOL requires that Form 5500 be filed every year. Entitled "Annual Return/Report of Employee Benefit Plans", the form is used to file all employee benefit plan information to the DOL. Generically, the form outlines the characteristics of the plan and its operations including: the plan name, information about the plan administrator, the number of participants at the end of the plan year, how the plan is funded, or benefits are provided, and any specific features of the plan such as an employer match.

Yet, what is amazing to me is that some firms do not take the violations they report on their own Form 5500 filing serious. Does the hiring of more than 1,000 additional auditors to inspect employee benefit plans not scare you? With some 650,000 qualified retirement plans in the United States, it's only a matter of time before they get to you. Moreover, with their recent online filing system called *E-fast2,* every financial statement, which is attached to Form 5500, is public information. This means that anyone with a computer can review any plan's Form 5500, which includes the DOL auditors!

The role of a fiduciary is important one. But it also requires an acute knowledge of the responsibilities associated with the role. But fear not, this book has been written and is designed to create "The 401(k) Road Map." It will educate you on how to build a plan that is prudently compliant, process driven, and an effective means of employee retention and attraction.

Chapter Two

Why Hiring Your Friend, Relative or Neighbor as your 401(k) Advisor is a Bad Idea

I recently injured my shoulder and wanted an evaluation from a doctor. I called my good friend who is a medical doctor (with a specialty in anesthesia), for some guidance. He immediately referred me to a non-surgical sports medicine doctor for an evaluation. After a consultation and a couple of months of treatment, I am thankfully pain free. But that's not the point. Both men are medical doctors having attended medical school and completed all their residency requirements and medical tests before embarking on private practice. Yet, one has a specialty in anesthesia and the other has a specialty in sports related injuries. Two completely different areas of practice, yet both are medical doctors. An analogy more closely related to my point considers the typical Chief Financial Officer of a corporation, which perhaps might be you, the reader. Most are licensed as Certified Public Accountants but their level of expertise comes from the auditing of financial statements of businesses, and not necessarily on the nuances of taxes. In fact, come tax time, they may hire another CPA to do their individual tax returns each year as this is not their forte. Again, both are CPAs, yet one CPA may hire another for a more specific expertise. So why is it that companies tend to hire

7

their relative, friend or neighbor to handle the ERISA compliance and fiduciary management of their retirement plan when they have little or no experience in doing so? Why aren't plan sponsors looking at their vendors the way they would select a specialist in medicine or income taxes?

The answer, while somewhat simplistic, and perhaps even a bit naïve, is that they just don't know any better. The defined benefit/defined contribution landscape has changed significantly from a regulatory perspective since The Economic Growth and Tax Relief Act of 2001 (EGTRRA). In fact, included in almost every piece of legislation passed since 2001, has been additional burdens of prudence, compliance and fiduciary standards. As the old saying goes, "This is not your grandmother's retirement plan anymore."

What used to be a hand out to the personal financial advisor, friend, neighbor or relative of a business owner as an additional gift of fees and commissions, can no longer be the standard. The rules have changed for financial advisors, beyond simply picking a bunch of investments and collecting commissions. A qualified 401(k) financial advisor is well versed in ERISA regulation, offers an in-depth consultative fiduciary process and offers un-biased education and investment advice to participants.

But what defines qualified? Historically, the answer may have been found through a psychological theory called behavioral finance. Simply put, the theory suggests that we make irrational financial decisions when we should be rational and make rational decisions when we should be irrational; or in other words, when it comes to making financial decisions, we do the exact opposite of what conventional wisdom tells us we should do. I will expound on this theory in a later chapter, but for the moment I suppose it could explain why business leaders in fact hire their friends, neighbors or relatives to manage their retirement plans. They are making an irrational financial decision without specifically knowing if a financial advisor is an experienced intermediary. In keeping within the rules of ERISA and following their requirements as a fiduciary, this could turn out to be a bad idea.

Moreover, in today's regulatory world, a resume is critical. While the financial services industry is a "who do you know" industry, Trustees of retirement plans need to instead understand the "what is it that they actually know" about the advisor that they are talking to. Like the example of the medical doctors earlier, plan sponsors need to understand what the advisor does and does not know about retirement plans and its compliance.

A trusted retirement plan intermediary, in addition to his or her own knowledge base, serves as a quarterback to the retirement plan. It is their job to recognize an issue and to advise and/or consult with the appropriate professional to solve it. To beat a dead horse, a non-specialized financial advisor will not only not be able to recognize a potential problem or issue, but it is more likely they will not have the specialized knowledge to know where to go to solve it.

Plan sponsors often find it necessary to seek third party assistance to help meet their fiduciary obligations regarding retirement plans. When soliciting a financial advisor, the goal is for that advisor to be able to advise and assist in acquiring the right product mix along with the appropriate professionals to further make the plan both compliant and successful. Thus, using a financial intermediary that regularly works with retirement plans can help reduce the risks to the plan sponsors because they know the typical processes involved, the experts to solicit for advice and how best to document the process along the way. In fact, a plan sponsor or fiduciary is better protected from liability risk when they have sought, obtained and considered expert advice.[4]

To further an earlier reference, the ERISA "prudent man" rule has been interpreted by the DOL, as well as the courts, "to act in a procedurally proper manner using an objective standard"[5] This rule requires that plan fiduciaries engage in a process to evaluate the quality and suitability of an investment, act consistently, and exercise independent, i.e. un-biased, judgement when making decisions regarding a plan. Failure to adhere to these standards, could constitute a violation under the rule and trigger the penalties and fees discussed earlier. What is critical for plan sponsors to understand is that lack of familiarity with investing and investments is not a defense. A fiduciary that selects investments will be judged as if that person has all the necessary knowledge to make that decision. If the fiduciary does not feel that they have the necessary qualifications to make decisions in compliance with this standard, DOL guidance and the courts have ruled that they have an obligation to seek qualified outside assistance. In the end, though, and regardless of the quality and level of the advice, the decision rests on the primary fiduciary of the plan.

Beyond necessity, there are several advantages to using the services of a financial advisor with respect to the management of an ERISA governed retirement plan.

An experienced retirement plan advisor will have a process aligned with ERISA regulation. This will involve a strong working knowledge or expertise in plan design, fund selection, ongoing investment management and advice. As will be mentioned repeatedly, it is about process and not the performance of the investments that get plan sponsors into trouble. In addition to navigating a process and helping to make better financial decisions, utilizing the services of an experienced retirement plan financial advisor may provide the plan sponsor or other fiduciaries an additional layer of protection from the liability associated with ERISA compliance. In fact, showing and documenting a fiduciary process has worked very well as part of a defense against a DOL audit.

In most cases, the plan sponsor typically has a financial background and may have some experience in making investment decisions. However, I will argue that such experience is somewhat limited in nature. At the end of 2014, there were over 14,000 mutual funds in the United States.[6] It is highly possible that even a sophisticated CFO will not have enough of a knowledge to be able to discern amongst these choices. Moreover, the amount of investment choices that are available has become so vast, that most financial advisors use some sort of software that establishes baseline investment criteria to be able to not only evaluate a fund against a benchmark or peer, but to also whittle the available options down to a manageable number, using that same set of criteria. Financial advisors can also create sample fund lineups. This becomes critically important with compliance with yet another regulation, ERISA 404(c). This specific section of the law permits employees to direct the investment decisions of their own retirement accounts. However, many employers often overlook a big portion of this rule. The critical piece of this legislation is that employers that comply with 404(c) can shift responsibility for poor investment results to plan participants. In short, 404(c) offers a "safe harbor" for plan fiduciaries to mitigate liability for investment losses suffered by plan participants who self-direct their investments. This means that employers will not be legally responsible for their employees' investment mistakes.[7]

To qualify for this relief under ERISA Section 404(c), the plan fiduciary must provide participants the chance to:

- Choose, from a broad and diverse range of investments, how their accounts will be invested, and
- Exercise control over their own investments within their individual accounts

The question begs: Does a fiduciary have enough knowledge to be able to offer the appropriate broad range of investment options that allow investors of all ages and risk profiles to make well-educated self-directed investment decisions?

Let's suppose the plan fiduciary did have that knowledge and expertise in these areas, that alone, while it may comply with ERISA 404(c), may not be enough procedurally, to comply with the ERISA prudent standard rule.

If I have not convinced you yet why selecting your friend, relative or neighbor as your 401(k) advisor is a really bad idea, let me offer one more important factor to consider: What does the financial intermediary's resume actually show for experience? According to the DOL and most related court decisions, a plan sponsor and a plan fiduciary have the responsibility to select the intermediary with prudence.[8] In order to comply, this process involves an extensive amount of due diligence on the capabilities of the intermediary to perform the role of an advisor on the plan to include, but limited to the following:

- Past experience, particularly with similar size plans
- Education
- References
- Disciplinary history
- Fees to be charged by intermediary

Once selected, the plan sponsor or fiduciary then has an ongoing obligation to monitor the quality of the intermediary and to employ a process to evaluate their performance on a regular basis. The most common place to start is with the advisor fee. As plans grow in size from both assets and personnel, the fee for the advisor grows as well. It is critically important to make sure that the fee is a market fee for the services rendered and that the monitoring of such is documented.

In addition, conflicts of interest may arise. Of late, the conflicts have revolved around compensation. An advisor is either paid directly by the plan through the plan assets and charges a percentage fee, or the advisor is paid by the investment companies whose mutual funds are in the plan's fund lineup. There have been multiple documented situations where advisors are compensated under both methods and essentially "double dip." There have also been many documented situations where advisors in commission paid accounts have directed plan participants into investments that pay a higher fee than other investments. Both situations are prohibited and need to be watched by the plan sponsor or fiduciary.

In consideration of the many different regulations and how they can impact the compliance and the responsibility of a plan, it makes sense to not only hire a financial intermediary for your retirement plan, but to make sure that he or she has the extensive background to ensure that the hiring is an asset. An advisor's main function is to help shield plan sponsors and fiduciaries from the risk of ERISA liability by providing access to investment intelligence and a documented process that augments the prudence of the decision making. To be able to show a process based on sound financial thinking, will prove to be extremely beneficial in the event any of those decisions are challenged later be a plan participant, or by a DOL audit.

Chapter Three

The 10 Best Practices in Plan Design That Will Attract and Retain Your Top Talent

So far, I have explored the necessity to understand the importance of being a fiduciary and have hopefully convinced you of the need to hire well versed professionals to assist you with your plan. Logically then, the next step in the path of the 401(k) road map is plan design. In 2012, The Internal Revenue Service published the 401(k) Plan Fix-It Guide. In this bulletin, they address 12 mistakes that regularly appear in a DOL audit. The mistake they note *first* is titled "You Haven't Updated Your Plan Document Within the Past Few Years to Reflect Recent Law Changes." But I could change the title of this mistake to reflect an even bigger issue and more likely scenario. It should be titled: "You Haven't Updated Your Plan Document Probably Ever." But again, I ask you, why does this matter? Because if your goal is to create a benefit plan to attract and retain the best talent then you must craft the tightest and well thought out document to do so.

I recently purchased a "fixer upper" and while I do not have anywhere near the talent of some of the designers I watch on television, I do know that without an end goal in mind and a blueprint to get me there, my renovation will not only be a disaster, but will end up costing me way more than I budgeted for. Similarly, you can't simply build a 401(k) plan until you design the features and benefits that it will offer. The plan document is the blueprint necessary to construct the plan.

A carefully constructed retirement plan, whose design is monitored and maintained on a regular and frequent basis is the base, or foundation of a successful plan. In sticking with the housing analogy, it is that base that allows every other aspect of the retirement plan to be built from the ground up. But here is the key: You must first clearly define the actual purpose of the retirement plan. Many years ago, it would have most likely been a tax shelter for business owners and a personal pre-tax savings vehicle. However, in today's working environment it is a necessary benefit for employees.

Earlier this year, I spoke at a conference in South Florida for start-up technology companies. Florida, and in particular, South Florida, under the current political administration has been trying to become a technology hub. They have established incubators at many of the local colleges to mentor and to guide burgeoning technology companies to success so that they become robust companies in the area creating jobs and economic growth. It's a great idea, but it needs some fine tuning. Areas like Silicon Valley, Northern Virginia, and even Austin Texas and Massachusetts have long been established as places for technology cultivation. It is quite a lofty goal to attempt to convince the best programming and software engineering minds to leave those hubs and to come to Florida. There must be a compelling reason to consider a job change away from the epicenters of existing technology hubs to convince those prospects to relocate to Florida, which is still incubating. One great reason would be that the benefit package, especially the retirement plan, is better than the competition. And it should be if you are listening to your employees! The younger workforce of today is interested in benefits that go well beyond salary. Healthcare, retirement benefits and other non-salary related concerns are high on this generation's priority list. The technology sector is just one example of this new phenomena. Other sectors are facing similar situations. Therefore, the message to the myriad of CEO's of the technology firms attending this seminar was simple: Separate yourself from the competition by creating a workplace where your employees have a solid foundation of salary and benefits not only for today but also for the future. Build your non-salary related package so that it makes it difficult for them to go elsewhere, and the foundation to do this is through a first-class retirement plan.

A well-designed plan serves as a magnet to attract and retain key employees. But it does more than provide an economic benefit. It illustrates a commitment by an employer to its employees that they are concerned about their people and feel it is their duty to help them optimize their personal financial future. We poll all the 401(k) plan employees that we meet with so that we can always understand what is important to them and report that back to our employer clients.

Like everything else though, in order to keep up with the pace of change it is important to consider the following ten plan design practices:

1. The first is participant advice. In the past, many plan provider's chassis simply built a plan directly for the employer and kept a financial intermediary out of the picture to avoid additional fees. Instead they offered an 800 number where participants could call and speak to a different person every single time, that knows nothing about the financial make-up of the participant and attempt to tender guidance. That is so yesterday's news. There have been countless studies on investor behavior and they all yield the same result. The typical American does not understand investments and/or

investing. In fact, if you recall in a prior chapter the concept of behavioral finance, then you will understand that when it comes to investing we tend to "sell low and buy high" simply because we are driven by emotion and not rationality. But the most compelling finding in this research is that investors are just simply not very good at picking their own investments in a 401(k) plan. So, offer professional advice. Yes, there is a fee for the advice, but if the participant pool is asking for it, then they are willing to pay for it, so a fiduciary should provide it. When polled 68% of companies retain an independent investment advisor to assist with advice to the plan participants.[9]

2. The second design feature is whether or not to allow for loans. The new terminology in this regard is called leakage and it has become a very controversial issue in 401(k) plans. The ability to allow a person to change one's mind or to consider their 401(k) account as a savings vehicle that can be tapped into when needed, takes away from the long-term commitment of investing for retirement. However, there are issues that arise in our day to day lives and while it is not a perfectly sound financial strategy, allowing for loans does offer flexibility and options to the participants. According to the Plan Sponsor Council of America, 89% of all plans surveyed do offer the loan availability feature in their plan.[10]

3. The third design feature is whether to offer a company match. Typically, I see employers making that decision based upon the cost in dollars of what the match would be versus the benefit and long term goodwill that could be built with the employees. While there are no standards to the actual quantity of a match, unless the plan has a safe harbor provision (more on that later), there are many ways to skin the match cat. For example, a typical match is to contribute

dollar for dollar up to the first three percent (3%) of the employee deferral. In other words, if the employee defers three percent (3%), the employer will match three percent (3%). In most cases that 3% pretax contribution works out to be a net wash to their take home pay when factoring in all the taxes. In other words, the 3% a participant contributes pre-tax equates to what their net take home pay would have been if they had to pay taxes on that amount. But what if the intent is to get the employees to defer as much as possible for retirement. The company could offer a stretched match where they offer twenty-five percent (25%)of the first twelve percent (12%). The employer still has the same level of match at three percent (3%), but has encouraged the participant to save even more to maximize the employer match.

4. The fourth design feature is to offer automatic enrollment. Again, relying on the concept of behavioral finance, research has shown in 401(k) plans that there in an inertia to do nothing if a participant is required to do something. In other words, if we rely on the participant to complete enrollment documents or to sign up for a retirement plan online, there is a risk that they will revert to the behavior of doing nothing. Automatic enrollment has reversed that concept. It is a behavioral based plan design feature that is becoming more of a rule rather than the exception. In fact, it is offered in over 50% of the plans polled in that same study by the Plan Sponsor Council of America. By enrolling every employee automatically into the plan upon eligibility, a plan sponsor not only gets the employee saving immediately for retirement, but it takes away the behavior of not completing the task to enroll. It also goes one step further to combat the behavior. Automatic enrollment forces the employee to "opt out" to stop the contributions, meaning that to not

participate, they are forced to act. This simple step has resulted in significant increases in plan participation rates. Once an employee sees their net paycheck and realizes that it includes the retirement plan contribution, they tend to remain in the status quo and not "opt out."

5. Similar to automatic enrollment, is the fifth best plan design practice called automatic escalation. This concept has also helped employees save more for retirement. Under this concept, on the anniversary date of enrollment into the 401(k) plan, the amount of contribution is automatically increased by one percent (1%) and is done so subsequently in every year thereafter until some limit is set as a capacity. This systematic increase has proven to be successful, as the typical participant will hardly realize the difference in the wallet.

6. The sixth best practice is automatic re-enrollment. This feature serves a couple of different purposes. The first is that creating an enrollment every year re-engages those that are not participating to reconsider and my research has shown that this procedure does translate to higher participation rates. A second and more meaningful benefit of this feature is that it re-balances an employee's account based upon their age into an investment matrix that may be more appropriate than the actual investment matrix that they have currently selected. American Century Investments completed an analysis of employee investments and plotted the results on a scatter gram. In the study, it showed that the oldest aged participants or, those closest to retirement, were invested significantly more aggressively than they should be and similarly by comparison, the younger workforce with the longest length of time to grow their retirement balances were invested much too conservatively. My research has shown

that when most employees enroll in a retirement plan and select their investment options, they seldom make changes to the investment options, if at all. The automatic re-enrollment feature can re-allocate each participant account to an age based asset allocation model, or target date fund, which is best suited for the employee's age. This way those participants with the least amount of working years are the most conservative and those with the most amount of working years are the most aggressive.

7. The seventh best plan design practice is instant eligibility. The idea that employees need to wait for some period before they enroll in the plan is slowly becoming outdated. As part of the design, there is a distinct difference between salary deferral and enrollment in the plan. While it is completely logical for employees to obtain some period of eligibility before they can start participating in an employer match, there is no reason to prevent employees from immediately rolling their assets from a former employer into the current employer's plan. By allowing employees to rollover prior employer retirement plan assets into the current plan, despite not meeting the eligibility for salary deferral encourages the employee to keep their accounts consolidated. It also helps to prevent the "out of sight out of mind" effect whereby employees lose track of prior employer 401(k) accounts and presumably stop watching or managing those assets.

8. The eighth design plan feature is to offer a Roth option. While a very complex topic that covers not only finance, accounting, politics, national debt and the future of taxes, I am going to address how it relates to plan design and save the other topics for another book. For starters, understand this: There is a place in your 401(k) plan for both traditional and Roth options and both should be offered as a feature.

The simplest way to describe the differences between the two is through the timing of income taxes. With the Roth 401(k) feature, the participant pays taxes on their income first, and then makes contributions to the retirement account using the net after tax proceeds from each paycheck. With this option, the entire balance of money in the account grows tax-free including any increases in the portfolio due to market growth. In addition, because taxes on the principal have been paid up front, there is no requirement to ever take a distribution from a Roth account

By contrast, contributions to the 401(k) using the traditional method are made with pre-tax dollars. In this scenario, the contributions are made into the retirement plan first, using the gross proceeds from each paycheck and taxes on these funds are paid when the money is withdrawn in the retirement years, thus the money grows tax-deferred. If at the age of 70 ½ is reached without any withdrawals, the Government will require a minimum distribution to begin to make tax payments. The rationale here is that the IRS has never collected any tax dollars on the contributions and at age 70 ½ the time has come.

9. The ninth best practice that was described briefly in chapter two is compliance with ERISA section 404(c). To reiterate, this specific section of the law permits employees to direct the investment decisions of their own retirement accounts. However, many employers often overlook a big portion of this rule. Employers that comply with 404(c) can shift responsibility for poor investment results to plan participants. In short, 404(c) offers a "safe harbor" for plan fiduciaries to avoid being liable for investment losses suffered by plan participants who self-direct their investments. This

means that employers will not be legally responsible for their employees' investment mistakes.[11]

To qualify for relief under ERISA Section 404(c), the plan fiduciary must provide participants the chance to:

- Choose from both a broad range of investments.
- Allow employees to choose how their accounts will be invested
- Allow each participant to exercise control over the assets in their individual accounts

10. The tenth best practice is to make sure that as a plan sponsor you select a Qualified Default Investment Alternative ("QDIA"). The DOL regulation regarding QDIA's became effective in December of 2007 to provide some relief to plan sponsors governed by ERISA. Historically, when participants enrolled in a 401(k) plan, but did not elect an investment, the contributions would be placed into a money market fund and except for some modest amount of interest, the funds would have no other ability for growth. The regulation regarding QDIA's changed this default. The rule states that in the absence of an investment decision by the plan participant, the plan sponsor steps in and makes the investment decision by placing the investment into the QDIA. The DOL defines a QDIA as an investment fund or model portfolio that seeks both long-term appreciation and capital preservation through a mix of equity and fixed income investments.[12]

While offering a QDIA is not mandatory, it does provide benefits to both the employer as well as the employee. For the employer, it reduces fiduciary exposure, reduces the concern that participants may not have a level of understanding of investments, and increases the chances of a more robust retirement. For the employee, it simplifies the investment decisions and provides a suitable long-term investment.

Chapter Four

Selecting a 401(k) Provider is No Different than Selecting a Hotel

So, I hope by now I have convinced you that your role as a fiduciary is not only an important one, but that it's also critical in your role to engage the appropriate intermediaries to assist in the management of a 401(k) plan. Logically, this book has followed a flow of next steps in the 401(k) road map. Once you choose an intermediary, the next step would be to select that vendor. However, with literally dozens to choose from, where do you begin?

I advise my plan sponsors to begin thinking about the selection of a 401(k) chassis the same way that they would select a hotel when on business or leisure travel. There are so many hotels to choose from, that most of us establish a set of criteria to help render a decision, and probably do so, without even know we are doing so. Hotel options range from limited service, no frills hotels that are usually not centrally located and offer lower rates, to five-star hotels, that have the highest level of service, amenities, and expensive linens. There is also everything in between. For example, when I travel, I typically stay in a suburban area and I prefer my hotels to include internet, parking, breakfast, a restaurant/bar, and in the slight chance I may use it, a fitness facility. Using the latest in travel search engines, I can filter these preferences into my search and whittle down my choices to a reasonable number. From that reduced list, I make my selection.

Selecting a 401(k) vendor follows a very similar path, albeit the criteria is different. There are the very limited service providers that offer a low-cost alternative, those that offer a high client touch and dedicated customer service teams, and providers that offer everything in between. In the past, a plan sponsor would receive proposals from the market and would simply select the lowest cost, but the landscape has changed. Employees are asking for additional services to be included in the plan, prompting the plan sponsor to request that they become a feature of the plan. Some of the services include: dedicated financial guidance, phone apps, and a well laid out user-friendly web site.

Let me be clear on vendor selection from the outset. First, there is no best provider on the street, but there is a best provider to meet your needs as a sponsor. Second, there is no absolute regulatory rule that the cheapest plan is the best plan. In fact, you can interpret ERISA to read that the process and justification of the process is more important than simply the cost.

I recently met with a growing technology company that had put a 401(k) plan in place a couple of years earlier. At that time, they were essentially a startup technology firm with a couple of dozen employees and felt that it was important to offer a benefit. There was however, no conversation and coordination as to how the plan would be designed (see chapter 2) or the actual role and responsibility of the fiduciary (see chapter 1), so the client hired my firm as the financial intermediary (see chapter 3).

At our first meeting, I explained to the team that just like the computers of today, what was built as a retirement plan a couple of years ago, can quickly become outdated and create the need for validation or replacement. I also explained that as part of their role of fiduciary, the DOL specifically says that a process of review should be written, established and used over time periods that are deemed appropriate. The guidance has not specified an exact schedule of when to do so, but rather, that it must be done and documented as to how frequent it will be done. Moreover, common sense would suggest to a C-Suite executive of a company, that vendors should be reviewed frequently anyway. In this case, though, besides the fact that the plan had never been reviewed at all, there were other compelling reasons to evaluate a change and the reasons were simple: The company was growing in personnel, the desires of the participants were changing, and the benefits they offered needed to be more reflective of today's participant needs in order to attract and retain their talent. I tasked management to build a committee, using several plan participants that would create both the quantitative and qualitative decision drivers of the plan. They needed to create a wish list of features and benefits that the plan would offer and a committee of peers to outline what was important to them so it would be included in the plan design. Once this was completed we could begin the process of finding the right vendor to fit the need.

Most of the providers in the marketplace offer very similar sets of their standard services. In comparison to my hotel example, they all offer a place to sleep and shower. However, a good fit is finding the provider that can accommodate the most important points of the wish list. Often this is carried out by issuing a Request for a Proposal (RFP) or for the less formal, a Request for Information (RFI). They are as important as with any other vendor a company considers, as they are the only way to compare the offerings of each.

Typically, the RFP/RFI is broken down into several sections, each addressing specific areas of importance and while I could pen an entire book devoted to the RFP process, I will briefly address some of the important sections:

A good opening section includes a brief overview of the company and the objectives including any important service standards to be expected. However, this section also asks for the overview of the vendor as well. Questions such as: How long have they been in the 401(k) business? How many plans do they administer? How many plans are in the company sector? And, what is their service model for a customer of the company's size?

The next section should relate to the vendor's fiduciary process. Are there any current or pending litigation or administrative actions against them? How do they receive their compensation? Do they revenue share with other vendors? What is their policy about sharing client or account information with a third party? What types and amount of errors and omission/liability insurance do they carry? What are the credentials of their administrative staff?

The investment section should address what I believe is one of the most critical pieces of a successful retirement plan and that is open architecture. This means having the ability to be able to invest in any fund regardless of the management company that runs it. A sound retirement plan should offer no investment options that can be deemed as a proprietary investment. For example, vendor "A" should not <u>require</u> the plan to invest in certain vendor "A" investment choices. In other words, 401(k) chassis' also serve as investment companies and often they require the plan to use their specific and proprietary funds. Instead, the investment section should proffer the best available options in each asset class regardless of the management company. Other items to consider: Does the vendor have a maximum number of investments allowed in the plan? Are there limitations to the types of investments available? What types of information about the investments are available?

Service is becoming the tiebreaker between vendors as of late. Based on surveys I take every year; the vendors have had to change their service offering to meet the plan participant desires. On-line enrollments and smart phone Apps have become the norm. Client education and retirement planning tips and advice are at the top of the page when the participant logs into the website. Dedicated service teams manage each client for continuity. However, the level and quality of service is like the hotel example. The lower priced plan providers will offer less customized and dedicated service than the higher priced full service providers.

The most recent addition to the RFP process is the addition of a section on cyber security. Lest we forget, we are dealing with personal information on an ongoing basis. It is critical that vendors have a plan to conduct periodic risk assessments to identify cybersecurity threats, vulnerabilities, and potential business consequences. Insist that your potential vendor provide documented policies and procedures as to how they protect your employee's personal information.

Selecting a vendor for your plan requires careful thinking, strategy and a lot of patience. A well-defined set of objectives will help to alleviate the stress of knowing what you are actually buying. However, understand that just like most other facets of a business, the 401(k) plan needs to evolve and adjust to the current times. A RFP/RFI should be modified and re-issued on a regular basis. If nothing else, it will keep the current vendor competitive.

Chapter Five

Enroll. Participate. Save.
The 3 Keys to Maximizing Your Employee's Retirement Readiness

According to the Social Security Administration website, the current law in place that governs the amount of benefits paid to retirees may have to change. In the year 2034, the payroll taxes that the Social Security Administration has collected and will collect will only be enough to pay out as a benefit, 79 cents for every dollar of scheduled benefits.[13] More simply put, over your entire working career, you are currently investing into a system that is going to pay you less than you have put in. It is a bad investment.

The reason the Social Security System has gotten to this point is because we are living longer forcing them to have to pay out for longer periods of time. A man reaching the age of 65 years old, based on today's life expectancy tables, can expect to live, on average, until age 84.3 years old. A woman reaching the age of 65, also based on today's life expectancy tables can expect to live, on average until age 86.6.[14] If you would like to know more about your own life expectancy, The Social Security Administration, has a great tool on their website called the life expectancy calculator and here is the link:
https://www.ssa.gov/oact/population/longevity.html

So why am I telling you all of this? Because, the findings of The Employee Benefit Research Institute, suggest that nearly one half (47.2 percent to be exact) of Baby Boomers are simulated to be at risk for not having enough resources in retirement to pay for basic retirement needs and for uninsured health care costs. The number is very similar for Generation Xers at 44.5 percent.[15]

Retirement readiness typically refers to being financially prepared for retirement, or the degree to which an individual is on target to meet his or her retirement-income goals so that the standard of living enjoyed while working is maintained after retirement. If the statistics above prove to be accurate, then most employees will not be "retirement ready."

The U.S. Department of Labor's "404a-5 Regulations" state that plan sponsors have a *duty* to promote financial literacy to the plan's participants and a duty to educate them on how they may save and invest through their plan. Participant advice in the form of "safe harbor" non-fiduciary education will protect plan sponsors against any potential fiduciary liability as a result of the advice. In fact, plan sponsors who improve the retirement readiness of their plan participants, can avoid additional risk, liability, and consider such advice as an employee attraction and retention tool.[16]

What is the difference between those who are projected to have enough money in retirement and those who are not? In addition, and equally as important, what can those who are expected to run short in retirement do to improve their retirement readiness? The answer is simple and I bet you already know it: participation in an employer-sponsored 401(k) plan. The best part of a 401(k) plan is that the contributions are tied to your payroll so the money comes out of your paycheck without you seeing it, and we all know that if we do not see it, it never existed anyway, right? This is forced savings at its best. With the automatic enrollment feature mentioned earlier, most participants do not even realize a difference in their net paycheck, yet they are saving for retirement.

How do you become retirement ready without sacrificing putting food on the table for your family or by making unrealistic goals? You follow a simple yet disciplined approach using the following three steps:

Step one is to determine a rate of savings based upon your total household income which includes your spouse or life partner. Retirement industry experts suggest that men should save between 10-12 percent of their annual income each year and that women should save between 12-15 percent of their annual income, again because women have a longer life expectancy. But to most people that seems like an awful lot of money. I typically tell participants that when I began my career, the job market was very tight, the economy was in recession, and despite being a college graduate, I had an annual salary of $19,000! Nevertheless, I was told of the importance of saving for retirement so I began by saving 1% of my annual salary, roughly $190 per year, which equated to $3.65 per week. Surely, I could figure out a way to save to $3.65 a week. I mean I had just graduated college and learned how to live on Ramen Noodles. But my thought process was that every year I was to expect a cost of living increase of approximately 2-3% of my then annual salary. So, if I were to increase the amount of my savings by an additional 1% per year, I would be able to increase the amount I save for retirement and get a raise as well, without having to sacrifice the standard of living in which I was living at the time. I kept doing this for 10 years and before I knew it, I was achieving a realistic savings goal without ever feeling the pinch. An even better example is what I refer to as the Starbucks example. For those of you latte lovers, think about this. If you gave up (heaven forbid), two Starbucks cravings per week at roughly $4 per visit, and continued doing so over a 30-year time horizon, at an 8% annual rate of return you would have over $50,000 saved in the bank. Think about that. For those that do not feel they have the means to save, a mere $8 per week can turn into almost $50,000 during your working career. Mathematically its gets even better. If that $8 per week can become $80 per week, the total becomes almost $500,000! It is not as difficult as it appears. The following link is also a great place to help you to determine if you will have enough to live on in retirement:

http://money.cnn.com/calculator/retirement/retirement-need/

However, suppose you just cannot part with your coffee. There is still hope. I often tell participants that when they want to lose weight, they need to count their calories (and I'm very careful how I present this.) If you take in more calories than you burn, the recipe for weight loss does not work. Same analogy can apply to saving. If you spend more than you make, you won't be able to save. But try this. Keep track of every dollar you spend every single day for one month. I think a couple of things will happen: The first is that you will be sick to your stomach to learn how much money is thrown away every month at things you cannot believe you spend money on and the second is you will realize what you can cut out of your financial diet to help you to be able to save. Take those savings and apply them to a payroll deduction into your 401(k) and you are well on your way.

The second step involves time. For those of you who are music buffs, in 1964 The Rolling Stones released a song called "Time Is on My Side." Little did they know that not only would that song become their first Billboard top 10 hit in the United States, but it would also become a mantra for saving for retirement! Mathematically and statistically, the greater the length of time to invest, the better the financial outcome will be. Let me give you an example. There is a mathematical algorithm called Monte Carlo Simulation. The algorithm is a collection of outcomes based upon the data that is entered. As the name suggests, it was created for the casinos in

Monaco to help determine the probabilities of the house winning versus the players, and it has been used for financial modeling since it was created in the 1940's. The model runs thousands and thousands of probable outcomes in a matter of seconds. Therefore, if you were playing blackjack with eight decks of cards, the formula could calculate the likeliest outcome based upon every hand that was dealt. The results of the mathematical outcomes helped to establish the rules of the game, as it gave the house (the casino) better odds. However, there is another element that became evident in this computation and that was that as more time passed, the higher the probability of success became for the casino. In other words, the longer a gambler sits and gambles, the chances to lose increase dramatically. In today's gambling environment, the average person sits at a blackjack table for 44 minutes, which explains why places like Las Vegas can afford to build $1 Billion dollar hotels and still make huge profits.

Nevertheless, why do I spend so much on gambling? Because when it comes to saving, you are the casino. You are the house. The longer the length of time you allow your investments to work, the better the probability of favorable outcomes. As John Bogle the founder of Vanguard Investments once said about investing, "Time is your friend; impulse is your enemy."

You will always have more saved for retirement the sooner you start to save. Consider this: investors that wait until their 40's to begin saving, should <u>double</u> the amount saved compared to those that started in their 20's and they still will not have as much. For example, if you started saving for retirement at age 25, putting away $2,000 a year for 40 years, you'll have around $560,000, assuming earnings grow at 8 percent annually. Now, suppose you wait until you are 35 to start saving. You put away the same $2,000 a year, but for three decades instead of four, and earnings grow at the same 8 percent per year. When you are 65, you will wind up with around $245,000 -- less than half the money!

While time is critical to success, so is having the proper mix of investments and having the discipline to stick with them and let them work. Mitigating risk is essential in the management of assets.

Step Three involves the savings process. Within the last few years, the most popular investment choices in retirement plans are Target Date Funds. These funds are a fully diversified portfolio of investment holdings that use age based formulas to mitigate risk. Their popularity has skyrocketed because they are simple to understand, simple to use, and because they are eligible to serve as a Qualifying Default Investment Alternatives.

The term "Target Date Fund" implies simply that. Each fund has a number associated with it and that number is the closest year, from the current year, in which the participant will turn the age of 65. The Fund is managed based upon that time horizon. The longer the length of time until age 65 the more aggressive the portfolio invests and it repositions gradually to a more conservative portfolio as the fund approaches the "Target Date." The participants do not have to manage the nuances of market conditions, nor make allocation changes. All of this is done for them. As coined by the prolific inventor Ron Popeil, it is literally "set it and forget it" for the participant. Mitigating risk through diversification, using either a Target Date Fund, or a custom-built portfolio, will help to address the growth necessary to sustain a standard of living in retirement.

It is not difficult to save for retirement, then is it? All it requires in a small amount of discipline, a consistent contribution, and time. Most important though, is that it is never too late to start.

Chapter Six

How to Effectively Minimize Your 401(k) Administrative Work Load

One of the bigger complaints I hear when talking about 401(k) plans is that administratively they are difficult to manage and require more time that perhaps, CFO's, HR Director's and payroll departments would like to spend on them. But again, this stems from not having the proper knowledge and advice from the intermediaries involved in the process. As you learned in Chapter Three, good, sound plan design can not only attract and retain the top talent, but it can also make the administrative portion of the business that much easier. But it still bewilders me, how little attention plan sponsors pay to the DOL rules and regulations regarding 401(k) plans.

One of the problems that I see most frequently, is a failure of the plan sponsor to remit contributions and loan payments into the 401(k) plan in a timely manner. This violation is known as a deposit timing failure. The DOL regulations define and state clearly that an employer must deposit employee contributions and loan payments in the 401(k) plan on the earliest date those amounts can reasonably be segregated from the employer's assets. In other words, the employer must make every effort to deposit the deferrals promptly with each pay period.

Through the Freedom of Information Act, I queried the DOL Form 5500 filings, to see how many companies reported having a deposit timing failure in year 2014. There were a reported 30,601 plans that had deposit timing failures in that calendar year.[17] While that may seem like a huge number to you, and believe me it is, what is even more astounding is how simple it is to ensure that this problem never exists at all, yet almost 31,000 companies are not doing it.

The DOL does however, make a distinction between small and large plans. If a plan has fewer than 100 participants, the deposit deadline is the seventh business day after the amounts are withheld from paychecks. Also, participants in a 401(k) plan are always defined as anyone with an account balance, as well as eligible but not contributing employees.

In plans with more than 100 participants, the employer will almost always be required to deposit contributions and loan payments more quickly. In most cases, employers are required to make the requisite deposit within a day or two after payroll.

As easy as it was for me to cite the number of failures of this regulation, imagine how easy it is for the DOL auditors to find out as well. Does my audit discussion ring a bell? Failure to identify and correct late deposits may result in penalties. Late deposits are treated as prohibited transactions, which are subject to excise taxes. Moreover, depending on the severity, late deposits may also be considered breaches of fiduciary duty and could result in personal liability.[18]

But the solution is simple and all that is required is to *integrate* your payroll with the custodian of the 401(k) assets. Payroll integration, by industry definition, is a salary-deferral feed connected through technology to a company's retirement plan. Historically, when a company ran its payroll through a third-party vendor, the payroll vendor would send a file back to the company showing the allocations and dollar amounts for each participant's 401(k) deferrals. The plan sponsor would then have to manually input, or upload that file to the recordkeeper, wherein lies the issue of deposit timing failures. It's that last step of having to upload one more file when the payroll department's to do list is overwhelmed as it is. When this laborious task goes on the back burner, the issues of timely contributions kick in. But somewhere along the way, the stone ages ended and technology took over, and this issue was solved. But, again, some 31,000 companies have chosen to continue to write in pencil, use adding machines and upload 401(k) files. I think you get my point.

There are two kinds of payroll integration and it is important to make sure you ask your provider which one is offered:

180° Integration – occurs when the data flows automatically from the payroll provider to the 401(k) plan recordkeeper. However, and as I recollect from geometry class, 180° is only half way, so the data does not flow back from the record keeper to the payroll company. 180° integration creates significant efficiencies and elimination of timing errors and data entry error because the payroll provider's software pushes the data directly on behalf of the plan sponsor to the custodian.

However, its gets even more efficient. 360° integration occurs when data flows both ways and the software of the payroll company and the recordkeeper speak to each other. The importance here is that while the payroll provider pushed the funds to the recordkeeper as with 180° integration, the 360° integration goes one step further. When an employee logs on to their account and changes their deferral amount, this information gets pushed back to the payroll company and eliminates yet another menial task of having to update the payroll system. Think of how important this becomes if your company has a large number of employees.

A second key ingredient in the 401(k) plan that helps to lower the administrative burden is to appoint the third-party administrator of the plan as the 3(16) administrator. Section 3(16) of ERISA states that an "administrator" is either "specifically so designated" by the plan document and in the absence of an appointment it is the plan sponsor directly.[19]

A plan administrator has more duties than what would appear on the surface, and I would imagine, in every case, more than any trustee would have signed up for. The defined contribution/defined benefit landscape is constantly evolving with rules and regulation and it is the job of the administrator to make sure that all the information gets incorporated into the plan document and disseminated to the participants. For example, when ERISA 408(b)(2) became effective, administrators were tasked with the additional responsibility to furnish participant specific fee disclosures in accordance with this new rule. But there are other tasks as well. Some are menial tasks such as processing loans, distributions, and hardship withdrawals. While other tasks are more significant and carry significant obligation such as being responsible for filing the Form 5500 and preparing the documents for a 401(k) audit, if required. The administrator has the responsibility to make sure the plan maintains its tax-qualified status and to make sure that it operates in accordance with the plan document. Failure to administer and comply with these obligations is a personal and not a corporate liability and the sanctions can be financially crippling.

But, there is hope. Plan sponsors of late are outsourcing some of their administrative fiduciary responsibilities related to their role as administrator by hiring their third-party administrator to be registered as the 3(16) administrator. In fact, as an additional revenue source, third party administrators have been absorbing a clear majority of the administrative tasks involved in running a 401(k) plan. It is a no brainer. The plan sponsor acting in their capacity as administrator does not have the time nor the experience to know what to do, when to do it and how to monitor it. However, the third-party administrator does have that expertise. For example, I have a client that has several hundred employees and for a small fee (a couple of thousand dollars per year), they can eliminate some liability but to also shed some of the menial tasks. Keep in mind however, that while an appointed 3(16) administrator will take the fiduciary responsibility of the tasks it takes on, such as the timely filing of a correct an accurate Form 5500, it does not fully alleviate you from all liability. The plan sponsor is still a fiduciary and is still responsible for the duties of that role.

That being said, below is a sample of the some of the tasks that one third party administrator will provide when engaged as the 3(16) administrator:

- Prepare, sign and submit 5500
- Loan review, approval, and processing
- Distribution review, approval, and processing
- Annual nondiscrimination testing
- Assume liability for DOL and IRS compliance testing
- Preparing and producing all mandatory notices including 408(b)(2) and 404(a)(5) with optional mailing services
- Take on liability for day-to-day operations
- Mandatory Notices including safe-harbor
- ERISA required annual participant fee disclosure
- Summary Plan Description (SPD)
- Statement of Material Modification (SMM) and annual Summary Annual Report (SAR)
- Terminated Participant Force Outs
- Termination Distributions Approval and Distribution
- In-Service Withdrawal approval and distribution (if applicable)

- Qualified Domestic Relations Order (QDRO) review, approval, segregation
- Annual profit sharing contribution calculations (Integrated, New Comparability, Pro-Rate)
- Annual match and Match true-up calculation
- Eligibility tracking through select providers
- Loan approval process
- Loan payoff calculation and processing
- Loan default notification and processing of distribution
- Required Minimum Distribution Calculation

Remember, this chapter was about creating administrative efficiency. So have I gotten your attention? I am willing to bet that most of you did not even realize the number of tasks involved in running a 401(k) plan until you saw some examples of the responsibilities you could eliminate! By simply integrating your payroll and outsourcing administrative responsibilities to a 3(16) administrator will not only make your job much easier, it will make your plan compliant with ERISA and reduce the risk of audits and fines down the road.

Chapter Seven

Breaking Down the Four Components of Cost

I recently had a home inspection completed on my house and it turns out I needed to replace the roof. To me, evaluating a roof contractor is kind of like replacing your mattress. Since you can't see what is inside, you must trust what you are being told and take the leap of faith. But even beyond that, if you go from mattress store to mattress store all the manufacturers have changed the name or model number of the mattress so there is no way to comparative shop to evaluate the best deal. I thought about this as I was shopping for a roof contractor. My thought process was this: If I establish a scope of work that is similar for all the contractors bidding for my business, then I would be able to determine who the best vendor would be based on the bids. Moreover, I did not select the least expensive bidder, but instead selected whom I felt was the best overall value based on the criteria I established. In fact, there are several steps to the process of replacing a roof and because of local building codes, all roofing contracting follow very similar methodologies of installation. The same theory applies when looking at the fees and costs of a 401(k) plan.

As I explain it, there are four components of the total fees of a 401(k) plan and each one of those fees is used to pay for the services rendered in administering the 401(k) plan. It is important that you evaluate each one independently to get a clear picture of the actual fees you are being charged.

The first fee covers the cost of the Third-Party Administrator ("TPA") and the Recordkeeper which are typically the same entity. TPAs are professionals who are versed experts in the regulatory aspects of retirement plans, and ERISA. It is their job to keep the plan in good standing with the IRS and DOL. Additionally, and as mentioned earlier, TPA's are also a great source to use when designing a plan from the beginning as they can take the desires of the company and make sure that they fit within the regulatory guidelines. Recordkeepers on the other hand, are responsible for managing the day-to-day operations of the plan. The assets of a 401(k) plan, that is, your contributions and employee matches, are held in an "omnibus account", in which investments are pooled together for all participants in the plan, as opposed to each participant having their own separate and dedicated account. The recordkeeper keeps track of which employee invests which amount into which account. They are also responsible for tracking participant contribution rates and investment selections, providing account statements, and maintaining records of outstanding participant loans. An ERISA recordkeeper works hand in hand with the payroll department or vendor, as well as, the plan custodian throughout the year to maintain an accurate accounting of the assets in the plan.

The fees associated with the recordkeeping aspect of the job are co-mingled with the fees charged by the TPA because in most cases, they are the same vendor. The first fee to consider is how the TPA is compensated and what is the fee that they charge for their services.

Some TPA's work off of a total revenue model and determine what their fees are going to be based upon how the total revenue is comprised. Fees to the TPA are earned in one of three ways: either as a base fee paid by the client, or through revenue sharing with the custodian of the assets, or by charging a per participant fee which is paid out of the assets of the plan. TPA's will evaluate all three in their entirety before they decide what to waive or discount. Some may propose a combination of the fees as well. The base fee is an annual charge to administer the plan as is quoted as a flat dollar amount. Revenue sharing occurs when the TPA has a contractual agreement with the custodian, whereby the custodian pays a portion of its fee to the TPA (this is very common by the way). The per participant charge is an annual flat dollar amount that is charged directly to the participant. As mentioned earlier, because the recordkeeper and the TPA are typically the same entity, this fee is typically quoted as one fee for both services. Thus, it is up to the plan sponsor and the 401(k) team to evaluate what the total compensation for the TPA amounts to, as well as, whether the fees are paid for by the plan sponsor or by the participants through the assets in the plan. It is important to look at all three ways they can earn compensation to best evaluate the competition. Lastly, recordkeepers and TPA's are the two types of vendors in a 401(k) plan that are not subject to any kind of government regulations, so it is important to understand their qualifications before relying on them as the source of all things fiduciary.

The custodian oversees handling the money. It is their responsibility to make disbursements from the plan, take contributions from the employees and to hold the plan's assets. They also make payments from the plan assets to the outside vendors including the TPA through their revenue sharing agreement, and the financial intermediary. Typically, a custodian is a bank, trust company or in some cases an insurance company. In the past it was very difficult to gauge the actual fees that were being charged for the plan by the custodian, particularly in the case of insurance companies, because they buried some of their costs into the fees of the investment options. However, with the enactment of ERISA 408(b)(2), any fee that is paid through plan assets, that is fees that are paid for by the plan participants, must be disclosed in writing, not only to the plan sponsor, but to the participants as well. For pricing purposes, custodians also look at the total revenue of the plan to determine the fee they will charge. Most custodians consider the average account balance which is calculated by taking the total assets in the plan divided by the number of participants. The higher the account balance the better their pricing will be. Their fee is quoted as a percentage of the assets that are in the plan and in some cases, they too may charge a per participant fee.

The third fee is the fee that the financial intermediary charges. Historically, there have been two ways in which a financial advisor/ broker is compensated. The advisor can either be compensated by the investment company that is within the plan, called a 12(b)(1) fee, or can be paid like the other vendors as a percentage of the assets in the plan. A 12(b)(1) fee is essentially a commission. I believe the term financial advisor and broker are reflective of the way in which compensation is earned. If you are being paid a 12(b)(1) fee by the investment company, you are being compensated by a third party and you are acting as a broker in the true essence of the word. Moreover, it is my opinion that since you are being paid by a mutual fund company there is an inherent conflict of interest because your interests could be aligned with the mutual fund companies that pay the highest 12(b)(1) fees. In fact, the Government agrees! In April of 2016, the DOL enacted in law yet another rule called the Fiduciary Rule. Without digressing heavily, the rule states that it is the role of all fiduciaries to act in the best interest of the plan participant, period. The rule also states that fees need to be level and consistent. When this rule first came out I wanted to understand it's implication. So, as I came across potential 401(k) plans to manage, I looked to see if the current fee structure being paid the broker was through a 12(b)(1) fee. I found that most of the plans I looked at, did. Then I dug deeper to see if some of the investment companies inside the plan paid a higher 12(b)(1) fee than others, and of course, some did. Lastly, I looked at the total assets within each fund and I can tell you that I was not shocked to find situations where the investment company that paid the highest 12(b)(1) fees to the broker had the largest balances of the plan assets. Now I am not pointing guilt at my financial brethren, but this certainly reeks of a conflict and is in total violation of this new rule.

On the other hand, a financial advisor, by my definition, is paid for advice, hence the term advisor. Typically, they are licensed as Registered Independent Advisors, and they charge a fee as a percentage of plan assets. Under this structure of compensation, the conflict of being paid by a third party and the conflict of earning a higher fee for one investment versus another goes away. In fact, I like to say that I am "mutual fund agnostic." Since my compensation is not tied to an investment product or investment company, I simply want the plan to have the best possible investment options available.

In the mind of many 401(k) advisors, (yours truly included), this is where the total fee calculation should end. However, many advisors choose to add the costs that the mutual fund managers charge to make the investment decisions on behalf of the participants to the overall cost of the plan. There are several reasons why this is done, and not one of them is for purposes of transparency or logic. There are two types of investment strategies in a 401(k) plan: active management and passive management. While I will expound on this in greater detail in a later chapter, the difference between the two strategies is that one employs a team of investment professionals to make decisions on the holdings within the mutual funds (active) and the other simply mirrors an index (passive.) So obviously, the investments that employ a team of financial minds making decisions is going to have a greater cost than the indexes that have no team of employees behind it. If a pricing structure was proposed that included only index funds within the investment matrix, the other aspects of the proposal, for example, the financial advisor fee, could be priced higher because the cost of the investment options are lower. This is flaw number one.

I have spent countless pages of this book describing the importance of being a fiduciary and acting in the best interests of the participants and to simply accept a proposal with all index funds because they are cheaper, assumes that all the participants in the plan are believers in passive versus active management. This is simply just flawed, illogical, and not realistic. As described in detail in Chapter One, a fiduciary has the responsibility to act in the best interests of the plan participants, period. The investment choices made by participants should be their decision only and it would be foolish to evaluate pricing of a 401(k) plan based on investment decisions they have yet to make. By only selecting index funds to be in a plan, you as a fiduciary, are forcing your participants to select one investment style while omitting another. This certainly cannot be construed as acting in their best interests. It is simply not a good policy for a trustee to evaluate the pricing of investments as a selection criteria without knowing exactly which options every participant is going to select and is the reason why I omit it from pricing. It does not keep the playing field level.

Chapter Eight

Cheaper Is Not Always Better: Active versus Passive Management

I'm a rabid college basketball fan. I will watch just about any game that I find on the television. Specifically, though, I focus on the coaches of the team. Why? Because the good ones will win no matter what team they are coaching. They have an innate ability to find talent and they have a consistent structure or formula to the way that they coach that talent. Managing investments and specifically, managing mutual funds, in concept is no different. A fund manager (or management team) uses their own formulas and their ability to select an investment that they believe will outperform another. Once that investment is selected they blend an allocation of that investment into an overall matrix. Following the basketball team analogy, each investment they select represents a player on the team. Once all the investments are selected the manager creates an allocation of each investment to create an entire portfolio. The goal is to have the portfolio outperform a benchmark which is akin to the basketball team beating its opponents.

But as referenced in the last chapter, there are two kinds of investment management strategies that can be used in a 401(k) plan:

investments that are actively managed by a team of professionals or investments that are mirror images of an index which are considered passive investments. While I can make arguments, both good and bad, for both styles of investment management, let me first explain the distinctions between the two.

I begin with active management and to further explain how it works I will use another analogy. Bill Parcells, the Super Bowl winning football coach of the National Football League once said "If they want you to cook the dinner, at least they ought to let you shop for some of the groceries." In other words, he was asked to coach a team of players using his style of coaching that was assembled by someone else. While those players may be highly skilled players at their respective positions, they were not specifically the type of players that Parcells fit into his formula. His preference would have been to use different ingredients to prepare his secret sauce. Active management is similar. Managers compile financial data on corporations as well as the financial markets and it's the actual data pieces that they collect that are used as their ingredients. What might be important data to one manager's model may not be a factor in another manager's model. They then take the data and create mathematical algorithms, to create an output. It's that output, or performance, by which they are judged. That output is the meal that they cooked using the data as the ingredients.

Proponents of active management tout the ability of the manager and their formulae to outperform a benchmark, net of fees, and thus can make the argument that their ability and model is a better product. There is a financial term that is often used in the industry, and most of us throw it around in conversations without ever describing what it means, and the term is "Alpha." Alpha measures performance on a risk-adjusted basis. Alpha gauges the performance of an investment against an index or benchmark. The additional amount of return that exceeds the index or benchmark is what is referred to as the

"Alpha." If an actively managed fund has a positive Alpha, then the manager is performing better than the index or benchmark that they are judged against.

The second important feature of active management is the ability to adjust for risk. Again, in financial jargon the measure of risk is defined by what is called "Beta." It is a volatility measure that gives an investor the ability to determine how the risk of the actively managed portfolio fares against its index or benchmark. If the fund is as risky as the index or benchmark, it will have a beta of 1. If, however, it is half as risky as its index or benchmark it will have a Beta of 0.50. Another way to view Beta is to think of it in the sense of how far a managed fund will rise or fall compared to the rise or fall of the benchmark. A Beta of 0.50 means that you can expect the actively managed investment to be as half as risky as its benchmark, so it will most likely lose half as much if the fund were to go down in value. A fund with a Beta greater than 1 is considered more volatile than the market; less than 1 means less volatile.

I am walking you through finance 101 to make a point. Active managers earn their keep by creating Alpha and lowering Beta. More simply stated, their goal is to perform better than their benchmark with less risk in doing so. However, actively managed funds get a bad rap in the marketplace because they have much higher fees than their passive investment counterparts. However, is that a reason not to consider them? Simply because they cost more? To me, the cost/fee evaluation has a flaw. It should be based on the value for the money. Think back to my hotels analogy. Depending on what you are looking for in terms of amenities and service will dictate the price or value. In addition, consider Bill Miller, the legendary fund manager at Legg Mason. His Legg Mason Value Trust Fund outperformed his benchmark, the S&P 500, for 15 consecutive years from 1991-2005. Moreover, his outperformance was after he was paid his well-earned fees! So, I pose the rhetorical question: If an active manager can perform consistently better than an index net of fees with less risk, does that not create value? I propose that it does.

However, the passive investors will disagree with me. Indexed mutual funds offer a very simple way to invest in broad segments of the market. Most of you are familiar with the Standard and Poor's 500, or more commonly known as the S&P 500. By definition, the S&P 500 is an index of 500 stocks that represent the leading indicators of the U.S. stock market and it serves as an indicator of the performance of the largest U.S. companies. The index is comprised of companies that are selected by a team of economists. The composition of the portfolio weighs each company's market capitalization, defined as the stock price of company multiplied by number of shares outstanding. The larger the company, based on market capitalization, the larger their weighting in the portfolio. For example, if General Electric represents 1.5% of the index, for every $100 invested into the index, $1.50 goes into General Electric stock. This type of investment does not have nor require a manager to run it so it is much less expensive than an active fund.

In fact, proponents of index investing will always revert to a financial theory to explain why indexing is better than their actively managed counterpart. The Efficient Market Hypothesis is a theory that states that because the stock market reflects and incorporates all existing information, it is deemed "efficient" and therefore it would be impossible to pick stocks that can outperform the market.[20] The theory further suggests that stocks always trade at their fair market value, making it impossible to find a stock that is under or overvalued. While this is a very powerful theory, the use of the word impossible is where there is a flaw. Bill Miller figured out a way to win for 15 consecutive years. What about all the television shows regarding residential real estate? If those homes, even in need of massive renovation, were purchased at their fair market value, then there would be no money to be made by the "house flippers." These television shows, as well as sound investment managers, consider the value proposition instead of the efficiency theory.

Therefore, what is the answer? The debate over passive versus active management has heated up lately and is considered amongst the greatest rivalries to the public. Think Manchester United versus Manchester City, Ali versus Frazier or Nicklaus versus Palmer. In fact, an argument should be made for the merits of both styles of investments. Yet, the two different camps are firmly entrenched in their conviction. Those that believe in the low cost, efficient market hypothesis of passive index management does not see the merits of having an active manager at all. Conversely, those that want potentially lower risk with the ability for more upside, flock towards active management and avoid the indexes completely. However, a case for a portfolio of both styles of investments can be made and candidly, is a solid financial decision. In the last chapter on pricing, I mentioned that it is not a responsible decision for a fiduciary to select an index fund, or an investment lineup because they are less costly. While, indexing may be the investment choice of the fiduciary, it may not be the investment choice of the participant. Some participants, me included, believe in the merits and the value of active management and believe there is a place for both styles of investment management in all plans. In as much as it makes sense for the fiduciary to think in the best interests of the participants, offering both styles of management will protect the interests of all participants. But it goes one step further, combined with sound investment advice, a portfolio can be blended using the two forms of structures to offer investment upside, risk protection, lower overall fees, and diversification that adheres to a participant's profile.

Chapter Nine

Ongoing Employee Engagement: How to Better Serve Your Participants

Whether you have figured it out or not, this book, this "road map" has followed a path. It is essentially the path that I have outlined to my clients as to how a plan evolves from its beginning to its never-ending end. Up to this point it has been about putting the plan together and making sure that all the features, benefits, and controls, are compliant with ERISA and at the same offer the best opportunity for the participants to succeed. But getting them to succeed is the next step in the process. While the value that you place on your intermediaries is important, listening to your participants is paramount. So, what are your participant's saying? Well according to the American Association of Pension Professionals and Actuaries (AAPPA), today's participants in a defined contribution plan do not simply want communication but rather they want individualized, customized personal advice.[21] They want to engage with professionals that can speak to their needs and to assist in mapping out a plan. We are going old school here! We have made such a deep push into the world of technology by automating as many facets of retirement plans as possible, that we forgot to consider service 101. Give the customer what they want and let them engage with a professional

51

that they can meet face to face, develop a relationship and trust with, and then feel comfortable talking to about their finances.

But let me back up for just a moment. We discussed automatic enrollment and briefly touched on automatic escalations in a prior chapter. The theory behind the concept was simple. If a plan sponsor goes ahead and enrolls a participant automatically into a 401(k) plan at a set minimum percentage, then all the employees will be enrolled and the job of helping them succeed towards building a retirement is complete. By automating the process, you have essentially forced the hand of the participant to enroll. According to Boston Research Technologies, while the participants in a survey did admit that without the automatic enrollment feature they would have probably not signed up for the plan, they also admitted that they would probably not sign in to a website, use the automated online tools available and most importantly make changes to what was initially set up. This includes increasing the deferral rate.[22] Moreover, most of the participants surveyed felt that because the company was enrolling them at a pre-determined rate, was all that would be necessary to give them the resources they need for an active retirement.

More troubling however, is that most participants don't realize the effect of automatic enrollment. Typically, when we set up a plan with automatic enrollment we set the initial deferral rate at 3% for the simple reason that generically, 3% equates to about what the pre-tax contribution would net if taxes were taken out. In other words, 3% of your gross wages will have little to no effect on your net, or, take home pay.

But how does the saying go "sometimes the best laid plans…"? While it was thought by experts that the best thing to do was force the hand of the participant by forcing them to save, in most cases, the strategy has backfired. They are deferring and saving less.[23] So, as I tell my plan sponsors, it is important to get them involved through automatic enrollment, but then a campaign needs to commence to not only keep them involved, but to get them to understand what retirement means and the importance of saving as much as possible.

For at least the last several decades, traditional 401(k) participant education efforts have focused on three areas: providing basic financial education, cultivating financial literacy, and providing 401(k) participants with the tools and data they need to make educated long term retirement decisions. All of this was typically done without the help of a financial professional.

But the data suggests that this formula is not only broken, it was probably flawed from the get go. A survey conducted in 2012 of over 1,000 401(k) participants revealed that 52% of respondents indicated that they didn't have the time, interest, or knowledge to manage their 401(k) portfolio.[24] Further to this same study suggested that 401(k) participants look to their plan sponsor to help them understand how to select investment choices and how to better understand how they work. This same study also suggested that financial literacy is a lofty goal—and a lot to ask of 401(k) participants. We see it in every plan we are engaged in. Most plan participants will not spend the time, nor care to learn enough knowledge to make sound financial decisions on their own.[25] Our industry is loaded with financial jargon that we can't possibly expect our participants to understand. In fact, I print out a definitions page for my plan sponsors that define the difference between a Large Cap Growth Fund and a Small Cap Value Fund. Herein then lies the flaw. We have been emphasizing financial literacy, yet, the audience with whom we are speaking are not in the position on many levels to comprehend or want to comprehend the language. Thus, sponsors concluded that they did their part by providing education while the participants were simply left scratching their heads.

What is it that we can do? The answer is to break down the financial education into visual pictures that the participant will understand. For example, when I build an investment line up for a 401(k) plan I always like to understand the industry sector for which my clients are working so that I can incorporate an investment that they will understand. I was recently working with a bunch of skilled nurses and while they are very astute in their field helping the sick and injured, they may not have the financial literacy we spoke about above. So, we put a healthcare mutual fund into the matrix of investments and spent the entire time talking about how a fund manager invests in the companies they know about and work with daily. Since they were familiar with the companies from their own career experience, this helped me to show them how investments selections are made and the results is that they are more engaged and interested. I also periodically present the "Starbucks slide". For those participants that do not think they can afford to save or do not understand the power of investing and compounding, I revert to the drinking of Starbucks coffee as an example. If you were to eliminate two cups of Starbucks coffee per week costing about $4.00 per coffee, and instead invested that at an annual rate of return of 8% for the next 30 years of your working career, those two weekly cups of coffee would be worth close to $50,000. Imagine what you could have if you saved even more than $8 per week. If it were $80 per week, it would be close to $500,000. By creating a picture that participants can understand, it is by default, creating an understanding of financial literacy. Engaging them to think about their decisions when ordering a Latte versus saving for retirement, is powerful, and it works!

The last piece to this study is what I find to be the most interesting because it is the most basic. Participants all expressed a desire to speak to a professional that can not only guide them but will listen to their needs and make recommendations accordingly. I always understood that to be the essence of how a financial advisor earns compensation in the first place.

Research has made it clear that participants are asking for individualized help and it is not difficult to implement. It just takes a small amount of diligence and discipline. In my practice, I create the opportunities for individual attention because I ask for and I set the meeting schedule with my plan sponsor. There are several times throughout the year that arranging for meetings make the most sense. For starters, I like to meet with my clients in January on the plan sponsor level so that we can review the existing investments in the plan and make sure they are still performing to the benchmark standards that have been set. Four times throughout the year, I arrange on-site meetings at the plan sponsor's offices so that any participant that is interested in speaking with me to discuss their investments can do so. Again, if they are asking for personal interaction we are providing it. I am often asked why we do not meet with participants on an even more frequent basis. The answer is that it does not make financial sense. Unless something catastrophic happens, making changes and reviewing on a too frequent basis can cause participants to want to "tweak" the account more than necessary. Investments need time to work and the patient investor will have a more disciplined approach to building a successful retirement nest egg. Think the tortoise versus the hare and the participant is the tortoise.

However, just because we are not on-site does not mean we are not available. In between in-person meetings we are available by phone, email, skype, video conference call and just about any other form of technological media that is available. But, it does not end there. Many of my clients tell me that they cannot meet with me during their workday because they are busy, they may want their spouse or other financial professional with them, or they are just not comfortable talking about this topic at work. To accommodate this request and further emphasize the importance of client education, I offer evening office hours twice a week by appointment. From my point of view, the more we engage the participants with advice and support, the more they are going to save for their future. In addition, we create value for our plan sponsors because we are an extension of proof that the company cares about its people by offering such a strong benefit. What a tremendous win/win for the company and its employees and an even greater win for talent acquisition and retention.

Chapter Ten

The Theory of Behavioral Finance – 5 Ways to Break Investment Regret

Although I briefly touched on this earlier in the book, I wanted to expand on the concept of behavioral finance, specifically as it relates to your participants in your 401(k) plan. Focusing on their thought process will not only help you better understand how to get the message out to them, but will help you help them in making decisions. In fact, I recommend that you share this chapter with your participants so that they can be better equipped with an understanding of how to channel their emotions and potentially prevent them from making poor decisions based on emotion.

It is a harsh reality, but studies show that our ability to make investment decisions is heavily influenced by emotions.[26] There is a piece of the brain called the amygdala whose job is to process the tidal wave of information that comes in front of it daily and look for potential danger. Without going deeper into the study of the human brain, simply understand that the amygdala regards all threats as accurate information.[27] With that in mind, the amygdala is also responsible for some of the mistakes that participants make when it comes to investing.

The first behavioral mistake that investors make is known as anchoring. Anchoring describes the tendency to rely on the first piece of information offered, the anchor, when making decisions. When deciding, individuals use that anchor to make future decisions regardless of other considerations, facts, or information. For example, my wife and I recently attended a show that we bought tickets for six months prior. When the intermission began in the middle of show, we looked at each other and decided that we did not care for the show at all and that we were bored. However, because we had purchased the tickets already and they were not cheap, we elected to stay for the second act thinking, "maybe the second act will be better." The point is, we were holding on to our anchor, which was clearly the price we paid for the tickets, with no consideration given to the new information provided to us, which was that we did not like what we paid for.

Similarly, emotional decisions are made using the anchoring effect without consideration of what is happening. For example, suppose that Company "A" had strong revenue in the last year, causing its stock price per share to shoot up from $20 to $50. Also, suppose that 50% of that company's revenue came from one customer and that customer elected to use a different vendor. Once the new revenue was reported without that large customer, the stock price reverted to the $20 price.

With anchoring an investor will tend to cling to the $50 stock price and determine that Company "A" is undervalued when the additional information suggests otherwise.

Availability bias is the evil twin to anchoring. Availability bias gives preference, or extra credit, to information that is most recent, available, and most memorable. Experts agree that memorable events that happen around us are magnified greater in our minds and cause a more significant emotional reaction. For example, I live in South

Florida and we very frequently read about shark attacks off the coast of our beaches. We are then warned by the news, and are fearful of going into the water because they are suddenly shark infested. The reality though, is that statistically, you are more likely to be killed by a part that has fallen off of an airplane, to which I am sure you find not likely to occur, than be bitten by a shark.[28]

Our availability bias is no different in the way we make investment decisions. In a survey conducted by Franklin Templeton Investments in the years 2010-2012, they asked 1,000 Americans how the stock markets performed for the year in each of those years. With what happened to markets in 2008, and more specifically how it affected their own personal accounts, almost 50% of those surveyed thought the market either had been flat or had gone down in value in those years. Yet, the reality is that from the lows in 2009, we saw one of the most robust runs in the value of the markets for seven years straight. Moreover, 2010-2012, the years surveyed were amongst the strongest.[29] But because of the bias of the pain felt in 2008-2009 they gave extra credit to the market losses and simply assumed that the subsequent years after the crash has similar losses.

The third behavioral mistake often made by investors is loss aversion. It is a simple conclusion to suggest that no one ever wants to lose, especially when it comes to money. This behavior though takes losing to another level. While loss aversion refers to pain investors feel when taking a loss, psychologists Daniel Kahneman and Amos Tverky estimate in their research that the pain from loss is twice is powerful psychologically, then the euphoria of a gain.[30]

In their analysis to prove this, they posed an experiment where participants were offered a chance to win a cash prize by choosing from two options:

1. A guaranteed win of $3,000

2. A 80% chance of winning $4,000 or a 20% chance of winning $0

As you can probably imagine, over 90% chose option number 1, the guaranteed win.

Then they switched the offer to look at it from the perspective of losing money:

1. A guaranteed loss of $3,000
2. A 80% chance of losing $4,000 or a 20% chance of losing $0

In this case, almost 90% of the participants opted for option 2, even though it included the 20% chance of losing nothing and statistically was a riskier option.[31]

The same can be said for our choices in investments. I cannot count how many times in the last several years that I was in front of a participant in a 401(k) plan who said "I need to be in something conservative because I can't live through another 2008!" It is now (as of the writing of this book,) 2016, some 8 years later. Participants though, are reeling in the loss from 8 years ago. It is yesterday's news. In fact, from the market low point in March of 2009, the S&P 500 has had a cumulative total return of over 234%. For those investors that are still feeling the pain from any loss in 2008/2009 have missed out on 234% of gains in the 8 years that followed. This is classic loss aversion behavior.

The fourth behavioral choice that leads to bad decision making is herding. Herd behavior describes how individuals inadvertently form a group to act collectively without any centralized direction. Think of how herds of animals group together or how fish swim in a pack. As an aside, while this behavior can be detrimental for investment decisions it can sometimes have positive outcomes. For example, my wife and I were recently in France where English, as a language, was relatively unknown and our French was limited. We were attending an event and were using public transportation to get there. Without knowledge of the exact location and without being able to communicate, we simply followed the largest crowd upon exit and made our way to our destination. Herding follows the crowd. In this case, it was to our benefit. However, when it comes to investing it typically leads to a market "bubble," or down turn.

Time and time again we have seen this where an investor will "jump on the band wagon." We saw this in the technology sector in 1999 and we saw it in the real estate crash in 2006. While there were very solid technology companies and very well priced real etate, not all technology companies were worthy of their price and the same for houses. However, as a herd, we needed to be able to buy something so that we could get our hands on the upside. In the stock markets, vicious market swings are typically tied to herding.

Take a look at the following graph. While timing of the market is almost impossible to predict, it is important to understand where an investor falls within the cycle. If you look to the left, the cross section is entitled "Smart Money." It is here where the institutional money managers may purchase an equity as the value, or upside, makes sense. As you move from left to right along the graph, you get to the section entitled "public." It is here where we as individual investors start to take notice of an investment and our herd mentality takes over. In fact I propose that for most of us, we bought tehnology stocks and real estate at or near the peak of this graph. Investors who follow the herd tend to buy high and sell low, the exact opposite of what conventional wisdom would suggest.

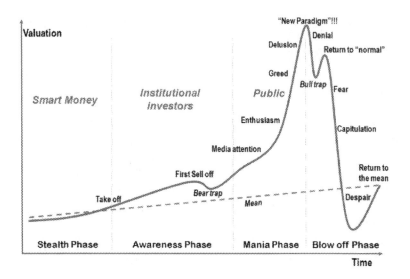

32

The last behavioral pattern that leads to investment mistakes is a theory coined by behavioral finance expert Richard Thaler called mental accounting. It essentially describes how people view money differently depending on: how it used, where it comes from, or its intended purpose.

I recently met a friend of mine for happy hour. I chose to drink the happy hour reduced priced house wine and he elected to have the full price rare scotch. When the bill arrived, I noticed that his scotch added up to almost $50.00 and my drinks were barely $12.00. Nevertheless, the interesting thing was during our conversation he explained to me that he drives 15 miles out of his way because he found a gas station that is $0.05 less than anything nearby. Spending $50 on drinks did not faze him at all, but look at the lengths he would go to save $5.00 on a tank of gas.

Investors employ mental accounting into their investment strategy as well. It seems that many investors have a strategy for a large portion of their portfolio but then have a "play account" where they can take bigger risks and not feel the pain if they don't work. This is not a sound strategy. All money, regardless of the account, belongs to the investor and regardless of where it came from, it should be part of an overall financial strategy. Another classic example is the tax refund. How often is it considered "found money" and spent on something like a vacation or something lavish. The truth is that a tax refund is simply a return of the excess money you let the Government use for the entire year.

Psychologists have studied the behaviors of why we do what we do, especially as it relates to making financial decisions. When plan sponsors, as well as participants are armed with the knowledge and understanding of what makes us tick, this information can often allow us to change our behaviors to the positive before making a drastic regrettable decision. In doing so, the goal is to avoid buying tech stocks in 1999 and houses in 2006. The theory of behavioral finance is extremely complex and entire books have been published on this topic. But a basic understanding of its fundamentals further demonstrates your role in the future success of your participants.

Epilogue

The management of 401(k) plans has been a passion of mine for many years. To be able to put my process to writing has been an even greater joy. I hope you followed the logic of this book as a path of how to effectively manage a plan from cradle to its never appearing grave. While many of the opinions in this book are my opinions, I do hope that it has opened your eyes to many important facets of this awesome employee benefit.

Many thanks to my business partner and first cousin Steven Weitz; my college friend and business attorney Todd Stone of the Stone Law Group; my dear friend, colleague and editor Jennifer Lyndsey; Peter DeCaprio, Jason Lucas, Jeanne Prayther, Sarah Cavanaugh, Kurt Kriter; Chris Berno, Victor Nappe and Regina Walker of Chaos for their cover and webpage design; my business associates, partners, and valued vendors, along with the unconditional love and patience of my wife Michelle during this neurotic process.

End Notes

1 https://en.wikipedia.org/wiki/Employee_Retirement_Income_Security_Act
2 http://www.rebalance-ira.com/news/neraly-half-americans-surveyed-falsely-think-they-pay-zero-retirement-investment-fees/
3 www.DOL.gov
4 Federated Investors: ERISA and the Responsibilities of a Plan Sponsor (March 2015)
5 ERISA Section 404(a)(1)(A)
6 2015 Investment Company Fact Book. Investment Company Institute. Retrieved 2 November 2015.
7 http://employment.findlaw.com/wages-and-benefits/erisa-section-404c-faqs-.html
8 http://webapps.dol.gov/FederalRegister/HtmlDisplay.aspx?DocId=28806$AgencyId=8&DocumentType=2
9 PSCA.org/55th-annual-survey-highlights
10 ibid
11 ERISA section 404(c)
12 TIAA-CREF
13 www.ssa.gov
14 www.ssa.gov
15 www.ebri.org/publications issue#344
16 http://www.wagnerlawgroup.com/documents/WhitePaper_001.pdf
17 www.DOL.gov
18 Department of Labor, EBSA
19 DOL, ERISA
20 www.investopedia.com/terms/e/efficientmarkethypothesis.asp
21 Aappa.org/articleID6052
22 Napa-net.org/warren Cormier

23 ibid

24 "Bridging the Gap Between 401(k) Sponsors and participants": 2012, commissioned by Schwab Retirement Plan Services, inc. and Schwab Retirement Plan Services Company. A sponsor study was conducted by CFO Research Services and a participation survey was conducted by Koski Research

25 ibid

26 Kahneman and Tversky, "Mental Accounting Matters," Journal of Behavioral Decision Making, 12:183-206 (1999)

27 Franklin Templeton Investments. Time to Take Stock 2012

28 http://onlinelibrary.wiley.com/doi/10.1002/acp.2350090202/abstract

29 The 2010 Franklin Templeton Global Investor Sentiment Survey designed in partnership with ORC International

30 Kahneman and Tversky, "Mental Accounting Matters," Journal of Behavioral Decision Making, 12:183-206 (1999)

31 ibid

32 https://en.m.wikipedia.org/wiki/Jean-Paul_Rodrigue#/media/File%aAStages_of_a_bubble.png

About the Author

Peter is Managing Director of the Weitz Financial Group. He joined the industry in 2003 after spending many years in real estate development in Washington, DC. After several years working for a large retail wire house, he became uncomfortable with the inherent conflicts of interest at major brokerage institutions and Joined an Independent Registered Investment Advisory firm in 2009, opening its South Florida Office. In September 2018, he launched the Weitz Financial Group, which coincided with him being names by Financial Times as one of the top 401(k) advisors in the United States for 2017. A dual graduate of George Washington University, Peter holds both an undergraduate degree in business and a master's degree in Finance. His primary areas of practice include corporate 401(k) and defined benefit plans assisting plan sponsors with their investment, fiduciary, employee education, and compliance responsibilities as well as individual retirement planning and wealth retention. He has published several articles and spoken on numerous panels regarding ERISA regulations as they pertain to defined contribution and benefit plans and has been recognized as a top performer nationally in the 401(k) marketplace by several 401(k) plan publications. He also hosted a nationally syndicated weekly radio program on finance and investments.

In his spare time, he is very active in his community and currently serves on the Board of The South Florida Institute on Aging, a Broward County 501(c)(3) dedicated to addressing the upcoming challenges of an aging population. When not active in charity, he enjoys golfing with his friends, reading, cooking, red wine, and travel. He resides with his wife Michelle and their two rescue dogs Duke and Daisy in Fort Lauderdale, Florida.

Printed in the United States
By Bookmasters